THE BIG FLIT

Castlemilk's First Tenants

Castlemilk People's History Group

Available from
Alison Miller,
W.E.A., St Margaret Mary's Secondary School,
65 Dougrie Road, Castlemilk, Glasgow, G45 9NJ

Tel: 041 634 0292

Published by
The Workers Educational Association
Castlemilk People's History Group
1990

ISBN   1 870140 11 7

Map of Castlemilk

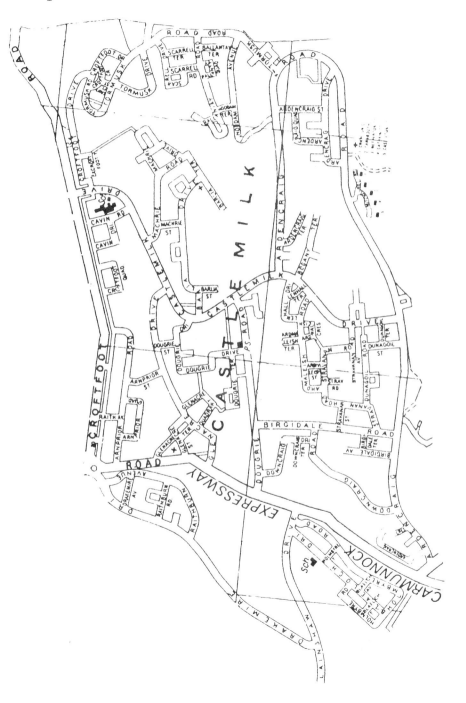

JOHN JAMIESON It is with sincere regret that the group records the death of John Jamieson, one of its founder members. The group are grateful to his wife, Millie, who has consented to have John's memories recorded in this publication.

ACKNOWLEDGEMENTS

The People's History Group would like to acknowledge the help, co-operation and support of the following people and organisations.

For their visits to the class with memories, photographs, information and stories:-

The late Iris McDonald - Castlemilk Tenants' Association
Mrs Mamie Murphy and the Rev. John Miller - Castlemilk East Parish Church
Mrs Mima Reid and the Clergy - St Margaret Mary's R.C. Church
Mr John McKechnie and the Rev. Robert Wotherspoon - Castlemilk West Parish Church
The Clergy of St Martin's R.C. Church
The late Mrs McGraw for the story of 'Frankie with the Hankie'
Jeanie Telfer - for her own story
Alex Erskine - for Photos
Rab Paterson for drawings
Nan Kerr - for the story of her work in Castlemilk Children's Home
Ken McLeod - Then Senior Development Officer, City Housing, Castlemilk
Elspeth King - The People's Palace
The Staff and children of St Margaret Mary's Secondary School

For their work and support in the production of this book:-

Pat Chisholm and MayMcLaughlan, who faithfully and patiently transcribed
our tape recordings and typed them up
COJAC and ADTEC - for use of equipment
Margaret Stewart of the Victim Support Scheme for help with the computer
Catherine Tait , Anne Fehilly and Irene Grahamof Safe Castlemilk for additional help
Ian Miller and Frank McAvoy - City Housing, Castlemilk for additional information
Paul Cameron - Community Education Service for design and layout
City Housing, Castlemilk for funding for the book and
Janice Currie for help and advice

Special thanks to:

Margaret Urquhart, the staff and committees of the Pensioners Action Centre for their
unstinting encouragement and support.

Finally we must thank Alison Miller and the WEA in Castlemilk, without whose wholehearted
support for the project and help in editing of the material, this publication would not have been possible.

Contents

INTRODUCTION

The recollections in this publication belong to the Castlemilk People's History Group. The group is funded by the Workers Educational Association as part of its remit to offer learning opportunities to all ages and all sections of the community. The group, formed in September 1986, are all members of the Pensioners Action Centre and the project is part of their attempt to establish the centre as a positive force in the community.

The group has enjoyed the use of written and visual archive materials. They have visited most, if not all of the Glasgow Museums for exhibitions appropriate to the project and passed through many public buildings and galleries. They are particularly grateful for the expert help of Elspeth King of the People's Palace in preparing photographs and other material for this publication.

They have enjoyed the musical knowledge of Adam McNaughtan. They benefited from visits to Glasgow District Planning Department and the Mitchell Library, Glasgow Room. Nearer to home, the group appreciated a visit to the Castlemilk Housing Involvement Project. They held conversations with the children of St Margaret Mary's Secondary School, with representatives of local churches, various clubs and with the late Iris McDonald of the Castlemilk Tenants' Association.

The activities encouraged the group to record the role they have played as founder members of the Castlemilk community. They moved as part of Glasgow's slum-housing clearance of the late 50's and early 60's or, in other cases, as hopefuls in Glasgow's policy of provision of housing suitable for the second half of the 20th Century. And, as tenants of one of the major peripheral housing estates in Europe, the members of the group have endeavoured to record their experiences with candour and humour. That record bears testimony to the hope felt by the people who first came to Castlemilk, that they were coming to a better life than the one they were leaving behind in the old tenements of Glasgow.

This publication is a small part of the total story of Castlemilk and it describes the beginning of an era that was already fast disappearing as the book was being put together. Recent years have seen much of the Local Authority housing stock taken over by Housing Co-operatives and by Scottish Homes. This has far-reaching implications for life in Castlemilk, and local people have already begun to feel the effects of the changes.

Not only has the housing situation been developing, but, before we succeeded in bringing the material in this book to the printing stage, several of the people featured in it had already died. Sadly, John Jamieson, a founder member of our group, is one of those, and we are very sorry that he did not live to see his memories in print.

Iris McDonald, who was interviewed for this book about her involvement in Castlemilk Tenants' Association, died in December 1988, after collapsing in a meeting at which she was presenting to the Castlemilk Partnership, the views of the Tenants' Associations on housing issues. The People's History Group is fortunate in having talked with her before her death.

In this interview Iris makes the point that "....it's a great pity.......that we do not stop to make a written history. We can only rely on memory". This book is the People's History Group's attempt to turn some of its memories into written history.

We hope it will encourage other groups and individuals in the area to record their own little bits of history, so that a more complete picture of Castlemilk's early days as a housing scheme may eventually emerge.

In the meantime, we hope that the stories set down here in "The Big Flit" are found to be of interest and, above all, enjoyed by all who read them.

Winnie Fox
WEA TUTOR
Castlemilk People's History Group
SEPTEMBER, 1990

CHAPTER I

Life before Castlemilk: Memories of the old Tenements

Most of the people who came to live in Castlemilk were leaving behind a 'room and kitchen' or even a 'single end in an old tenement, with no bathroom and a toilet on the stair. The kitchen was where you lived, cooked, ate and slept.

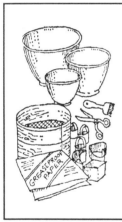

"I have very happy memories of our kitchen. I always thought of it as big. We had a chest of drawers with lovely brass handles. You never thought you were poor. Everything was always scrupulously clean."

"Everybody had a dresser with pots and pans on top."

"We had brass edging on the mantlepiece, where tea and coffee pots hung, though they were purely ornamental."

THE RANGE

The fire was a coal fire in the middle of a big black leaded Stanley range. On either side of this there was a cooking area. A one or two ring hob and a grill fuelled by gas piped from the gas lighting sat on the side of the range. And there was a penny meter for the gas. The oven was heated by the fire. If you wanted a very hot oven, you had to stoke up the fire. There was a lever you could move to let the heat through or lower it Behind the fireplace was a common place for mice.

THE BED RECESS

Because the bed was in a recess in the kitchen, you had to have it nice. People often had an Alhambra bed mat, paisley patterned and made of heavy cotton with fringes.

1

WASHING

People used to do their washing in the boiler house in the backcourt. Every tenant had a day and sometimes you only got a turn once every two weeks. You had to get up about 5 or 6 o'clock to light the boiler and it would take all day to do a washing.

If you did it in the house you used the sink with a washing board. There was a piece of wood at the side of the sink, and the wringer was screwed onto that. So the clothes were wrung out first on the wringer and then hung on the pulley in the kitchen.

Some people went to the 'steamie' to do their washing. It was hard work. You had to book your time on the steamie machine. You made a lot of friends. My man used to say, "When's your steamie pal coming up?" It was a social occasion, steamie day. Nowadays the social aspect of washing is gone; you have to find other ways of being sociable.

TOILET AND BATH

Most people had a toilet on the stair that you shared with all the people on the landing. There would be three families with an average number of six people per family - a total of about eighteen people using one toilet! There was no wash-hand basin and no plumbed in bath.

Children in back court, 1926.

"The big zinc bath was the family bath. It was about 3 feet long with handles at each side. We used it for taking the washing down too. Friday night was bath night and everybody washed in the same water'

Every Friday night the weans all used to get baths and my husband was on night shift. I'd get them into the bed recess and draw the curtains. A wee while later I'd shout "anybody want a meringue?" - When I got no answer I knew everything was OK and I'd jump into the bath.

CHAPTER 2

The Big Flit

NOTIFICATION FINALLY ARRIVES

I remember the day the card came through the door telling me I had a house in Castlemilk. That was in April 1957. I was all excited - I was getting A NEW HOUSE! I ran out and phoned my mother - I just couldn't wait. Then when my husband came home from work, he was over the moon too. We both went to the High Street housing office the next morning, but only my husband signed the form. He had to take a day off work and lost a day's wages but we didn't think about that! We also had to sign a form stating whether we wanted gas or electricity services. Water was connected and we were to get hot water from our coal fire. The electricity board could put in an immerser, but you had to pay for that yourself.

New tenants, Croftfoot Road, 1956

We got the missives for our house which gave us the regulations for payment of rent and rates and things like cleaning the stairs. We paid our rent every quarter, £8 it was. We only paid £1-7/- in our old house in Cowcaddens.

We got the keys and my husband took the two oldest girls to see the house that same day. They didn't know where to go, but it was a nice day and they got there somehow. We had three children and a baby of 9 months so I couldn't go to see the house just then - I thought it was awful far away. In fact, I didn't see the house until the night we moved in.

When they came back and said the house was on the ground floor I thought I was getting a back and front door you know - but it was a corner house with a big garden in Ardmaleish Road. They talked about the white sink in the kitchen and the BATHROOM - we only had a toilet on the stair. They were all thrilled.

All this was a very big step for us, you know. I was the only one of my family moving to the south side of the water, but I didn't like the house I was offered in Drumchapel where all my family were going. To this day I've been happy and I haven't regretted moving to Castlemilk.   ROSE McLEAN

WE ALL QUALIFIED

I QUALIFIED! March, 1956. I had been on the housing list for twelve years. On my son's 10th birthday, he became eligible to be considered an adult. My youngest boy was 2 years old. You had to come up to be at the allocation   of   the new houses. I wanted top flat, 2 up and I got it! I had lived ground floor before in a room and kitchen. We moved into our 3 apartment in Croftfoot Road in March. My husband and family were all delighted.
AGNES DICKSON

THE BUILDING WAS TO BE DEMOLISHED

We put our names down on the housing list when we got engaged in 1947. We were married and had a seven year old boy when the housing department said we didn't qualify for a 3 apartment new house. Then we heard of a family whose house in Moffat Street Oatlands, was to be demolished. We exchanged with them though we never actually moved into their house in Moffat Street.. We moved straight to their new house in Castlemilk and they took our rented house. We had to show our old rent book to the Corporation housing department to prove our rent payments were up-to-date and my husband was asked what his wages were. We moved July, 1956.

PEGGY MACAULAY

WE EXCHANGED WITH A FAMILY WHO STAYED ONLY ONE MONTH IN CASTLEMILK

I was staying in Elmfoot Street, Oatlands in 1957 with my husband and two girls. I had a nice house, 2 rooms and kitchen, the toilet was on the stair. Before I was married I stayed in a Corporation house in Logan Street, Oatlands, so I was used to having a bathroom. We took it quite ill having to go down the stairs to the outside toilet especially late at night or early in the mornings.

The woman I exchanged with hated Castlemilk. She was away from her family and friends. Her children had to travel to school in their old area because there was no schools. She just hated all the hassle. Her husband also had a long journey to work and bus fares added to their bills - it was like a second rent.

However, I didn't have these problems. My children were too young for school and my brothers and sister also came up to live in Castlemilk.

MAY MARTIN

THE BIG DAY: A MOVING TALE

I moved from Bluevale Street in the east end in October, 1955. Our building was to be demolished and all the tenants were moving on the same day. I had ordered the removal van but it broke down and didn't come until 9pm. My furniture was out in the street all day ... and down came the rain!

We got to Castlemilk in the dark and there was no light on the stair. We took the furniture up the stairs by the light of a bicycle lamp. I can't remember how long the removal took. It cost 30/-, I remember that!

We had no gas connected and no light. We couldn't even light a fire because the coal nest was missing!

I also had no bed. My bed was ordered and didn't come to the next day - but I had a mattress.

You had to depend on neighbours that day - being kind and giving you hot water and heating up your dinner. But everybody rallied round. You knew your neighbours because we all came together and moved up the same close or round about - so it didn't feel too bad.

NAN TIERNEY

I LEFT THE DINNER BEHIND

I lived in Moffat Street and moved up to Glenacre Drive in July, 1956. It was a dry day, a good day for flitting. The van belonged to a firm in Allison Street. They arrived at 9am. Our belongings were packed in tea chests. I had been gathering the chests from Cochrane's and Lipton's to store our stuff. Everyone had mucked in, especially my husband's brother. We had had to get up at the crack of dawn to dismantle the bed before the removers came. They packed the boxes in the van and off we went. We sat in the front with the driver. We had to direct him because he didn't know where to come. They unloaded the van and that was it.....
I thought! I went to get the dinner on and discovered I had left it behind!

I was lucky, my friend had stayed behind in my old house to lock up and give the keys to the family we were exchanging with. She had found the casserole in the oven. She jumped on the bus and took it up to us.

PEGGY MACAULAY

THE WARDROBE THAT DIDN'T FIT

I moved to Castlemilk from Polmadie in April 1956. It was midday as everything got piled in the van. I was quite excited, I think the weans had a rerr terr.

The men brought the furniture in. I had a utility bedroom suite. It was solid, with a great big wardrobe. It took a wee bit of manoeuvring to get it in so they dumped it in the living room. They took the beds and things upstairs. When the men left, my husband and his brother tried to move the wardrobe. They tried all ways - upside down, sideways, but it wouldn't move. Luckily my husband was a joiner. He took the whole thing to bits, marked each bit - left hand, back and all the rest - and carried it bit by bit up the stairs. He put it together again in the top bedroom. It's there to this day. I don't know what will happen if it has to get moved again - I'll leave it!

ISA ROBERTSON

'AND THE PIANO CAME TOO'

We had a piano in our house in Garngad Road. When we moved to Castlemilk in 1956 we had to make special arrangements with the removers to get the piano down 2 flights of stairs and then up 3 flights to our new house. They had special wheels and straps to do the job, but they must have been exhausted.

We kept the piano for quite a few years, but then I decided to get rid of it. I took a hammer to it - the dust was flying everywhere. My brother-in-law helped me.

MAY GILLEN

A DUMPLING ON MY KNEE

I moved up to Castlemilk in December 1955 and was the first tenant in my house. The houses were just new built. I stayed in Govan and when I came up to see the house, I took a 34 bus - I always called it a '34 shops' because it only came as far as Croftfoot - and I had to walk from there to Castlemilk Drive to see the house. And when we decided we would take a house in Castlemilk, they picked our names out of a hat to decide where we would be placed. I was lucky enough to get 52 Castlemilk Drive.

On the day I moved in, I came up from Govan in the removal van with a big dumpling on my knee. My aunt stayed in the same close in Clynder Street and, as we were coming out to come up to Castlemilk, she handed me this huge big dumpling to share with the driver and the men. The children came up later with Jimmy, my husband. Dora was the eldest; she was thirteen at the time and was at Bellahouston Academy and she still kept going there after we moved to Castlemilk. The youngest was the baby at four months. When I left Govan, my mother thought I was going to the other end of the world going to Castlemilk. She thought that was terrible.

MAMIE MURPHY

MY NEW HOUSE - THE THOUGHTS OF ISA ROBERTSON

I stayed in Polmadie Road, Oatlands with my husband, two boys and two girls. We had a two room and kitchen. I was delighted when I got word of my new house - a five apartment with a BATHROOM AND A GARDEN.! - oh the excitement! However, we had a family council and the kids all sat round the table with my husband and I. We discussed this because the rent for the new house was to be three imes the rent of the house we were in - But we decided to have a go.

Good Neighbours, Croftfoot Road,

The kids were delighted. They didn't want to be left behind. A lot of families were going to Castlemilk at this time. There was also the excitement of the brand new house. Our kids loved the Oatlands. There was great camaraderie there. But I think it was the idea of a new place, green fields and plenty of space.

For me I was going to have a kitchenette with a BOILER. I didn't need to go to the steamie or down the back-court wash-house. I also had a bit at the back to hang out clothes. A dream come true.

And then there was the bathroom - a luxury in your own house. You could have a bath, put on your nightgown and sit at the fire, go to bed whenever you felt like it all in comfort

The bathroom was to be great for the kids too. When they were wee, you could put them in the sink or a bath at the fire. As they got older it had to be the bath at the wash-house every Saturday.

Then there was the kids getting washed everyday. What a performance all greetin and moanin as they stood at the window where the sink was. We had to pull the blind down but we couldn't stop all the draughts. There was all the kettles of water heating.

They had privacy too - the girls were growing up - 12 years and 10 years and the boys were 12 and 2 1/2 years. If the girls were getting washed, they wanted the boys out of the room.

We soon made good friends in our new area. When we arrived, our neighbour called in to introduce himself. We remain close friends for over 30 years. Our neighbours on the other side were good friends too and had the same surname as ourselves.!

We worked together to fix the gardens - everybody pitched in. We planted potatoes and cabbages and carrots, blackcurrant bushes, strawberries and raspberry canes.

These early days were great times, full of excitement and happiness and hope.

HIGH LIVING

I was the first tenant in the high flats, Dougrie Place. I moved in with my husband in October 1964. We balloted for house allocation and got the 13th floor - we could have changed, but I'm not superstitious.

I really wanted to move to the high flats because they were in a nice spot, with a wonderful view. From my bedroom I can see Glasgow and the Campsie hills. From my living room I can see down towards Arran.

When it is stormy, it can be noisy. You can't hear the TV when the wind is high - but you get used to it.

There are two lifts in the flats, one that stops at odd number floor levels and the other which stops at even number floor levels. The lifts give very little problems.

The flat I have is a 2 apartment. I like the size. At the beginning, when the flats opened up, 2 apartments were mostly offered to people without families. The 3 apartments were for families.

In the early days, I found it a wee bit difficult to get to know my neighbours. We only met on the lift. Gradually I got to know more people. I got to know the people on my own landing - they were balloted the same time as myself.

The middle of the 3 blocks has a common room. In the early days the Tenant's Association used to organise socials - they were good. They are improving again.

I'm quite happy in my high flat and wouldn't think of moving.

NAN TIERNEY

NOBODY MOVED ON A SATURDAY - SATURDAY FLIT - SHORT SIT

It was considered bad luck. I often wondered about those folk who moved in, stayed for a wee while and then disappeared, leaving the house empty. There was always quite a few houses empty, brand new as well.

There was no amenities, no shops, practically no schools and extra bus-fares.

When people came to Castlemilk, there was a tremendous change to their lives. Some people couldn't take the shock. Others couldn't afford it. We were like early settlers. We needed an extra wage for bus-fares to get to visit our families, who were all away in another part of town.

Children had problems too. They had to be bussed all over to their old schools. Some kept up social activities in their old districts - the boys brigade for instance. That meant more bus-fares. A lot of women went out to work when their children got a bit older.

INA LYNCH

THE FLIT - FAMILY OR CO-OP

Flitting was a family affair then - all your relatives would help. Some would be at the new house sorting things out, and would have tea made and beer for the men.

The Co-op did a lot of removals in those days. They would bring big tea chests and everything was packed in. When you got to the other end, they even put down your carpets.

ALLOCATION OF NEW HOUSES

You didn't get to pick your new house. Your name was put in and lots were drawn to allocate you a specific house. However, people with medical reasons could be allocated ground floor houses.

LOSING FAMILY CONNECTIONS

It was sad to be moving away from the place where you were born and brought up and where your family lived, either up the next close or nearby.

CHAPTER 3

The Housing Department's Plans

THE BACKGROUND

In Britain in the 1940's and 50's there were massive amounts of building and a lot of thought put into what should happen. Around Glasgow, a plan was drawn up - the "Clyde Valley Plan" - in the late 1940's. This plan stipulated that Glasgow should try to keep within the boundaries that existed in 1945, and advocated that there shouldn't be any large schemes on its edge, but that places like East Kilbride and Cumbernauld should be allowed to develop. Glasgow Corporation was hostile to these proposals: it didn't want people to move away, possibly because it would make Glasgow a less powerful city. As an alternative to these proposals, there was talk of clearing housing areas like Mosspark and Knightswood and building really high density houses. Thus the alternatives were new towns or high density developments. Castlemilk came out as something of a compromise between these two positions.

STAGES OF CASTLEMILK

The early years of building in Castlemilk was around Arnprior, Glenacre Drive, stretching to the bottom of Castlemilk Drive. This happened between 1954 and 1955. By 1956, there was the beginnings of Ardencraig Drive, Bogany Terrace, the top part of Castlemilk Drive and down Tormusk Road. The last bits were around Birgidale, Downcraig, Dunagoil, Drakemire and Raithburn.

The earliest houses to be occupied were in Arnprior Quad, part of Glenacre, part of Dougrie Drive, part of Machrie between January and December, 1955. After that, around Arnprior, Croftfoot, Cavin, the bottom of Castlemilk Drive and a bit in Ardencraig Quad and Road.

DESIGN OF THE HOUSING

There was quite a bit of friction between the Scottish Office and Glasgow Corporation about the design of the houses. Glasgow Corporation stuck out for tenement type dwellings, possibly because they were under the impression that Glasgow people wanted tenements. There was no consultation with tenants over the planning of any aspect of Castlemilk.

A third of all the houses are built to the same design, the 'T' design with a big verandah at the front of the house. There are a lot of houses the same design in other schemes like Drumchapel and Easterhouse.

Castlemilk could have been spread out much more. Before World War II, Glasgow Corporation had bought all the land up to Carmunnock. But when Castlemilk was first built, people thought it w as beautiful. Most people had waited a long time to get a house and appreciated then greatly. People spent a lot of their own money and their weekends planting hedges and creating gardens.

Castlemilk Drive in Winter

THE HIGH FLATS

The multi-storeys were built in the 1960's and early 70's, at the same time as they were going up all over Britain. They became popular, because the Government was making it clear that it wanted system-built housing - pre-cast cement, rather than bricks and mortar

Walking to school over ground now Birgidale Complex. High Flats in the background

SOCIAL NEEDS

There was an assumption that families, rather than other groups, were to be catered for in this type of housing provision. The main priority was families from inner city areas, who had to be rehoused either because their houses were too small, or because they were unfit for habitation eg. the clearance of the Gorbals and Govan.

Until recently single people had to look to the private rented sector and there were no policies to cater for extended families.

THE EARLY ROLE OF THE HOUSING DEPARTMENT

Once the people had moved in, the Housing Department saw it's role as one of collecting rents and repair reports. The Housing Office used to be where Dougrie Unemployed Workers Centre is now, then it moved to Ardencraig.

No special training was given to Housing Department officials. Although there were more people then - the population of Castlemilk has been dropping sharply over the last fifteen years - there was a lot less housing staff. And those that there were, were at a junior level and provided a mainly clerical service.

Based on talk by Ken McLeod then Senior Development Officer with City Housing, Castlemilk.

View of Windlaw Farm from Ardencraig Road

CHAPTER 4

Early Days in the Scheme

THE HOUSE

We moved into a brand new house. It was very cold and took a lot to warm it up. The ice on the windows was 2" thick when we moved in. I think the budgie got a chill - it died shortly after.

The walls of the house were emulsioned. You were not to paint or paper for one year till the building had settled.

We didn't need a bunker anymore. The coal cellar was in the hall, next to the outside door. The houses in Glenacre Quad had a hatch from the landing. In some houses the coal cellar is entirely separate from the house - out on the stairhead.

JOHN JAMIESON

WHO THE HELL ARE YOU?

A man walked into our house one night, hung his jacket up in the hall and came into the living room to sit down. He noticed my husband sitting and Jim said, "Who the hell are you?" (Jim worked on night shift and I think he thought I'd been up to something and this was my fancy man!) "Oh Christ!", the man said, "I'm in the wrong house.

At the time we all moved in to the houses, they looked so much the same. When you came off the bus across the road, it was easy to walk up the wrong close. It happened to more than one.

INA LYNCH

DIGGING GARDENS

Every tenant in our bit had their own wee piece of garden. We all had 5 apartments. The land was already fenced off. We prepared the soil with help from neighbours. Everybody helped each other. We planted potatoes and cabbages and carrots. We planted blackcurrant bushes, strawberries and raspberry canes and made jam

17

every year. We also had a hutch with a pet rabbit in it.
ISA ROBERTSON

Digging gardens,
Croftfoot Road, 1956

The plots in the back-courts at Arnprior Quad were all divided. My husband and a neighbour fenced off our part at the close. We planted potatoes, carrots, lettuce and peas. (We never got to eat the peapods because all the milk boys stole them!) On the other side we grew flowers. We looked after these plots for quite a few years. We also had a drying green. The back-courts were all well looked after. Everyone was keen to keep the place tidy.

MARY DOCHERTY

After we got in, we began to get tidied up and my father-in-law was helping me dig up the garden. He dug out a whole pile of bricks left over from the building of the houses. And here, the Corporation folk came round and told him he would have to return the bricks. He says "I'm no returning no bricks; I've dug them out of the garden and they're staying there. You want the bricks, you come and collect them yourself" We dug up enough bricks to line the side of the garden up the path. Ornamental, you know!

The corner gardens were a big lump of ground; a hundred and thirty two feet of fencing round ours. Too much for anybody. That's why we moved in the end. We left it in good shape, but we were glad to get an upstairs house.

JOHN JAMIESON

We first moved into a flat on the ground floor in Glenacre Drive. My husband would look after the front garden. We didn't get the sun at the front so we put a hedge round the grass and kept it tidy. We weren't supposed to get a share at the back because we had the front plot, though we had a share of the drying green like everyone else.

PEGGY MACAULAY

Vegetable plot, rear garden. Arnprior Quad, 1957

We moved into our five apartment in Croftfoot Road. We had both a back and front garden for the very first time.

I had four children and soon my back door became the meeting place for all the kids. I would make candy and tablet and my husband would have a ball for them to play with.

We would sit at the front porch in the afternoon when the sun came round. We had the sun at the back all day long. Sitting at the front you would have a blether to folk as they passed and the kids would play at the back.

ISA ROBERTSON

We moved into a flat in Glenacre Drive in 1957. There was a plot for growing vegetables and a drying space. The rest of the space was for the kids to play in. They played with the children from all the closes that looked on the the back-court. It was communal. They played at 'shops' and other games. The children loved it. It was so open and with grass. In the old tenement back-courts, everything was divided by railings and there wasn't much light because of the high tenement buildings. Here everything was so bright, clean and green.

MAY MARTIN

"Castlemilk didn't get fog. It used to reach Croftfoot and lie there."

"Castlemilk has a lovely approach road (Carmunnock Road). The east end is nice where the nurseries are, with all the beautiful old trees."

KITCHENS, BATHROOMS AND BALCONIES

My second house in Castlemilk was in Birgidale Avenue (1966) and just like my first house, it was great to have a kitchen. In the other house in Oatlands you lived, ate and slept in the same room.

There was a cooker, a big washing tub, a sink, a drying cupboard, a larder and a broom cupboard. There was a gas boiler to boil clothes. Some people made dumplings in the boiler. There was a pulley for hanging clothes to dry. Later on we put in an electric immerser for hot water. We thought we were toffs when we set the table in the living-room.
PEGGY MACAULAY

Peggy Macaulay, in her kitchen, Birgidale Avenue

Joey the budgie and Ina Lynch, balcony, Ardencraig Road

My kitchen in Ardencraig Road had all mod cons. I cooked and washed in the kitchen. It was long and narrow and when I was at the cooker and the door shut and someone came in from the living room they would bump against me - but it was still great to have the separate kitchen.

We went "all electric" in 1964, did away with the coal fire and fitted an electric immerser.

We also had a balcony. We had a lovely view. We had the sun all day from early in the morning to late at night - lots of fresh air too. There was a farm opposite us in use. Many a time the cows would get out and run up and down the road. We would have to phone the farmer to tell him.

We had a budgie 'Joey'. We would take him out on the balcony for a wee while when the sun was shining, but he preferred the shade.

INA LYNCH

I always said to my friends after I came up to Castlemilk, that I had a bath once a year now whether I needed it or not!
JOHN JAMIESON

TRANSPORT

In the beginning most buses only came to the Croftfoot Roundabout. When there are bus strikes you have to walk. The nearest train station is Croftfoot or Kings Park.

> *"When there is a lot of snow the buses get stuck at Castlemilk Drive or Carmunnock Road."*

SHOPPING

We went to Croftfoot for shops, or bought from mobile shops. The vans charged extra and people had to pay through the nose. They also gave credit, but you paid back an enormous amount.

Milk and coal was delivered. This service was free and was ideal if you had young children. When I was signing the missives for the house, Perratt's (the dairy people) were there looking for orders.

Shopping wasn't easy. There were so few shops - mostly vans or a long walk to Croftfoot. Most people went back to their old areas to shop. It was difficult to change old ways.

"MY TRIP TO SHAWLANDS"
After moving to Castlemilk, as there wasn't many shops, I made a point of going back to Shawlands, (where we had come from originally) on a Saturday to do my main shopping. On this particular occasion, my son came with me. He had just got a new camera for his birthday, and he snapped me leaving the house, getting on the bus at the terminus, in Shawlands's with all my shopping then getting off the bus back home. It was a big trek every week.

DOCTORS/DENTIST/OPTICIANS/HOSPITALS/ CLINICS

Some people stayed with the doctors in their old homes. Some went to doctors based in Croftfoot. There were no surgeries immediately in Castlemilk. Doctors had no appointment system then. You could leave home in the morning with a sick child and not get home till early afternoon.

Nearest hospital is the Victoria which is used often.

In Arnprior, houses were converted into a clinic.Then a clinic was eventually opened in Ballantay Quad.

ENTERTAINMENT

If you wanted to go to cinemas or dance halls, you had to go out of Castlemilk. People made their own efforts to provide entertainment. Co-op guilds were very popular, they held dances and bus runs.

CHAPTER 5

Castlemilk Tenants' Association

Based on an interview with Iris Mcdonald, March 1987

I'm one of the first tenants in Castlemilk and, shortly after we moved in - that would be approximately 31 to 32 years ago around 1955 - we were canvassed round the doors and more or less everybody joined the Tenants' Association.

That may seem strange nowadays because, at that time, everybody was very happy to come out of the old tenements into new houses with facilities they had never enjoyed in their lives before. But Castlemilk was just in the process of being built. When we moved in, the houses were ready, but the pavements were totally unusable; there was no bus service; there were no amenities whatsoever. As I recollect, you didn't even have any shops in the scheme. They came as the scheme was being built, and then you got the shops at Machrie. There was very little except the houses, no schools to speak of. They had put down the houses and that was it. Certainly I am in no doubt that they intended getting round to the other things, but the Tenants' Association was formed in order to gee it up.

One of the founder members, an outstanding person, was Mrs Hamilton, and Frank Slater and David McWhinnie were also founder members. I was a young mother at that time, and out working and looking after the family. Although I was a member, I wasn't personally involved.

One thing I must say at this stage is that it's a great pity when someone asks for a rundown on what the Tenants' Association was, that we do not stop to make a written history. We can only rely on memory.

SUPPORT FOR TENANTS' ASSOCIATIONS

I would say that the Church was quite keen on getting the Tenants' organised. But Councillors - well one of the things you have to remember about attitudes at that time was that some of the Councillors were inclined to be a bit paternalistic. They still are, but more so then. They thought they knew best about everything and people were a wee bit in awe of them. Not so much now, and I'm very pleased about that.

THE WORK OF THE TENANTS' ASSOCIATION

The issues the Association was first involved with are the obvious ones - conditions in the area, lack of repairs, or whatever. There were obvious problems then, but they weren't so outstanding, because it has to be remembered that when we all moved in here, we were young, we had young families and our aspirations were different as well. What people are not willing to put up with today, they were willing to accept then. People were pleased with their houses. A lot of people put down estates like this. My house has no more faults than any other, and generally speaking, the houses are quite good. Of course, we now have problems which didn't occur then.

You had a lot of people moving in then who didn't like Castlemilk. No so much they they didn't like the people, but they had moved away from inner city areas, up to a place which didn't have a great bus service and they found they were away from the centre of things. Quite a lot of people drifted back within a few years to Govanhill, Townhead, Govan or whatever. They didn't like being so far out of the city.

CHANGING ASPIRATIONS AND GROWING PROBLEMS

Every decade people's aspirations change and things evolve. Where we were very happy at that time just to move into a house, now we have different kinds of tenants. One problem familiar not just to council houses but also in the owner occupier houses is a kind of gypsy population. We have moved from stable tenures and for about the last ten years we have this kind of gypsy attitude to housing. People move on and move on.

There has also been the development of problems such as dampness within the houses themselves. And over the past ten years there's been the escalation of unemployment within the area. I think that everyone who is a long standing tenant would agree that in the early days - the first fifteen to twenty years - there was very little unemployment. It was the exception rather than the rule. The aging of the tenants also brings its own problems.

Mary Docherty, back court, Arnprior Quad, 1956

ADVERTISING THE ASSOCIATION AND INVOLVING THE COMMUNITY

We have almost 10,000 houses in Castlemilk. If we were to leaflet all of them, the cost would be astronomical. We have done leafletting, not just us but other groups, and the response has been abysmal to say the least. We put posters up every month in as prominent places as we can. Again this is one of the things we suffer from in Castlemilk: we don't have enough places to put things up for public display so that people can see them. We have posters in the Library, Housing Office, Community Council. But we don't have what there used to be, specific corner gardens at various points round the scheme with a notice board in them. It wasn't a large thing, but it was a place where public notices could be put up. These have gone. Now you can go from the Arcade here down to the other side of Castlemilk, whichever way you go, and there is absolutely no place you could put a poster. You could go the length of Dougrie Road and there is no place. I have complained about this for years. I would like to see a large almost indestructible notice board.

This is not the total problem, though it is a problem. It is a great disappointment to me that we haven't managed to get more people involved in the Association. Again it is a sign of the times. We have an aging population. People in many respects, and who can blame them, are loath to come out at night . Then again the people who do become involved are also committed to other things. So, getting the people out has became increasingly difficult. The original Castlemilk Tenants' Association is still in existence and there's a lot of people who have been here as long as it has who still don't know about it. We meet and always have met on the first Monday of the month, except on holidays. That's always been it, and we still have people who don't know.

THE ROLE OF THE ASSOCIATION TODAY

The objectives of the Association are to safeguard the interests of the residents of the Castlemilk scheme. And to enlighten tenants on local and national legislation which affects them; to promote such activities as may be deemed advisable to foster the social and educational life of the community - which is why I'm here today.

When the Glasgow lease was re-negotiated in 1985 I was part of the negotiating team through the Glasgow Council of Tenants. I saw my role as making sure that that lease was the best people could have, and it is about the best one in Scotland. You can have a good lease but are still bound by the legislation around which it is formed. Our role has always been in that kind of situation.

In Castlemilk the most obvious role for the Association is in fighting for improved conditions in housing and the environment. The two go hand in glove. You can't say to people : "Here's a lovely house, modernised and everything in it". And you have a crappy backyard that's full of litter. I look at these backcourts with the bins stuck in front of the windows - most of them have no lids on. And the backs are small, too small. Large backs could bring a lot of pleasure to the people and the children that live in there. And yet nobody seems to be making any attempt to clean them up and make them fit for recreational purposes. That kind of thing is every bit as important to the person standing at the sink, washing their dishes - looking out at a nice bit of landscaping.

Those of us who have lived here for a long time will remember that we got gutters cleaned out regularly, closes painted and things of that nature, and that has just gone by the board. Because the number of houses that were built after that was so huge, we just couldn't keep up with that sort of programme. Buildings should be inspected - we referred before to dampness - if buildings were inspected it would be seen that some of the grouting between the brickwork had come out and was needing replaced. These are all the things we should be looking at.

NEIGHBOURS' or NEIGHBOURS

I would like to say that television is a lot to blame for peoples' disinterest. One of the worst things is that people are now more interested in Eastenders, Coronation Street and the Dynasty syndrome than they are in what is happening in their street. Some people will stand and discuss with great emotion, the problems of these fictional characters, and they don't know what's happening in the next close, or bother about litter. This gets me very angry and a bit frustrated, I have to say. But it's a sign of the times. I don't deny people entertainment, but it shouldn't rule your life.

Iris McDonald died in 1988.

Arnprior School, Primary Four boys

Glenwood School, First Year group, 1958

CHAPTER 6

Some Castlemilk Characters from the Early Days

FRANKIE WITH THE HANKIE

A character well remembered by the group is Frankie McGraw. In his eighties by this time and too frail to come himself, his story was told to us by his wife Mrs McGraw.

He would take out his hankie and wave it and get everybody into the singing. They all used to get up and march round waving their hankies.

"Frankie was a coppersmith to trade. He worked 50 years at it and what did he get for it - buttons! But he loved to sing: he spent most of his spare time singing. He went round all the clubs and social nights - St Bartholomews, St Margaret Mary's, the Monday Club - singing Joseph Locke songs and 'Your Cheatin Heart' and even opera like that Mario Lanza. It was the gimmick he had for songs like 'The Soldiers Farewell' that earned him his nickname, Frankie with the Hankie. He would take out his hankie and wave it and get everybody into the singing. They all used to get up and march round waving their hankies. He was a wee man that would keep things going. Suppose they were all sitting sleeping, he would soon waken them up! And in the middle of it all he would shout "What's my name?" and they would all shout "Frankie".He loved it.

He went round hospitals too with a concert party - all men from Castlemilk - and sang to all the patients. But it was his solo singing and his hankie that he was famous for. He used to get asked all the time to go to clubs and social nights. He would never let anyone down: even if it was snowing he would go. He's a wee man, only a tuppence halfpenny man, but he was very popular - popular with the women. And it must run in the blood, because my grandson, young Frankie McGraw, he was the disco king!"

Mrs McGraw has since died.

THE FIRST BOOKIE IN CASTLEMILK

I don't know his name but, before the shopping centre opened up, he stood in the spare ground. He took in lines there. He also had a man who came round Glenacre and, if you put a sign up in the window, he came and collected your line. You used to have to keep your eye out for the polis, because it was illegal! The line was just a bit of paper with a nom de plume on it. I think my husband's was 'Shoemaker': his father was a shoemaker to trade and he just used that. He came every day, I think, but I went with my husband's line on a Saturday. There was always a lot of people there and the women would all stand together. It's funny to think that now we can do lines by using satellite.

JEANIE TELFER

Jeannie Telfer was a well known character in Castlemilk. She sold newspapers at 4 o'clock in the morning at the bus shelter on Castlemilk Drive at Dougrie Drive. You couldn't get into it, the shelter was so packed at that time of the morning with people going to their work. A lot of them worked in the college and at that school facing the Victoria Infirmary.

At that time the papers - it was mostly the Daily Record she sold - cost 3d. Jeannie also sold cigarettes, though that wasn't legal, and sometimes even things like linen sheets, 3/- a pair. She would deliver papers too, to houses round Glenacre, Dougrie Street, Dougrie Drive, and shout people up for their work. The whole street could hear her, right through to Castlemilk Drive.

THE OLD WOMAN WHO LIVED IN A COTTAGE

Even after a good lot of the scheme had been built, there was an old woman, who lived in an old stone-built cottage, which faced onto where the bowling green is today - between Castlemilk Drive, Dougrie Drive and Dougrie Road. She had a fair bit of land fenced in at the back of the cottage, where she kept hens. Children from Machrie had to pass right by her cottage door on their way to the Dougrie Road School. There were beautiful snowdrops growing in her backyard - the only snowdrops around - and children would climb over the fence to pick them. If they disturbed the hens, she would come out and chase them with a broom. With her old fashioned clothes, living in a cottage with the scheme going up around her, she looked strange, as if she came from a different world. The children all thought she was a witch, of course.

But she held out for a good few years and stayed right there in her cottage. Who knows, maybe we owe her something. If she hadn't stuck it out all that time, the Corporation might have put houses on that land too and we wouldn't have had any kind of centre in Castlemilk.

34

CHAPTER 7

At Work in Castlemilk

For many people, moving to Castlemilk meant long bus journeys every day to and from work in other parts of the city. Few people found work in Castlemilk itself, but here are some who eventually did.

When my children went to high school, I went back to full-time nursing. I had done part-time work (2 nights) at Lightburn Hospital when the

children were younger. I started as a full-time nurse in 1966 in Windlaw Old Folks' Home (aged persons' hospital).

I loved the work. It was hard sometimes because I still had to come home and look after my husband and three children - but we managed.

I soon became a staff nurse and then deputy matron (I had been assistant matron in a convalescent home for children in Maybole just after I got married).

The home was mostly geriatric patients from the local district, south east Glasgow. I loved my work. I got on well with the staff and patients. It was different from when I was a young nurse. Everything now is more relaxed but everyone is looked after. You got to know the patients and their families.

When I was deputy matron, I had to do a book-keeping course, because I had to deal with pensions and wages. I retired in 1984 after 16 years in Windlaw.

SADIE MUIR

I worked in Malone's shoe repairs shop in the Castlemilk Arcade for a few years. It was the only shoe repair shop in Castlemilk. At that time all the shops were used in the Arcade. We had Boots the chemist, Taylors the chemist, Woolworths, Galbraith's, Co-op food and furniture, Clydesdale electrical, Terley's, Galls, Ladbrokes, 2 or 3 Shoe shops, Gas and Electricity Showrooms a Fish Shop, a Launderette, Menzies, a Wallpaper Shop, 2 City Bakeries and 3 Butchers. It was a very busy arcade, serving the whole area. Consequently, the shoe repair shop was always busy.

I had worked part-time in Lewis's before this, but because I had

Castlemilk Fair outside the shopping centre

a young family, I found it difficult. This job was full-time and local. So I had more money and less hassle for my family.

The shop also sold school bags and was very busy when the schools started with a' the Grannies buying school bags for the grand weans.

MAY MARTIN

I worked in Arnprior Clinic for 22 years. The clinic opened in 1955 and housed a baby clinic, school clinic, dentist and optician and doctors related to each

I moved into Arnprior Quad in July 1955 and noticed that the 'T' block house next to me was not occupied. I asked the workmen who were there what was happening and they said it was to be a clinic. They said if you want a wee job get right into the City Chambers and see about it. I  wanted the job because the money would come in handy having just moved house. We had a lot of new expenses.

I cleaned this building along with one other woman. I liked the company of the staff, the nurses when they came in in the morning, but most of all the job was handy.

The job was hard work too. We had to hump coal and scuttles up to all 3 stairs in the early days, there were fires on every floor. Later the clinic changed to gas. Cleaning changed too. You used to have to get down on your knees to scrub, then later we got mops. I enjoyed the job.

MAY SHIELDS

I had worked part-time in Cohen's factory in Shawlands when I first came to Castlemilk and stayed there for 10 years - I needed the money.

By the late 60's I got fed up with all the travelling especially in the winter when the bus can't get up the hill. So I applied for a job with the home help service and got a job based in Castlemilk. The office was based in Rutherglen when I started in 1972. I'd worked as a home help for almost 15 years when I retired.

The work was varied. When I started I did 4 hours every day with each patient. We washed, ironed, cooked and shopped. We did many other things over and above that we weren't supposed to do.

You got to know your patients personally, they treated you like a daughter. I had one patient for 9 years and she got on to me like a mother would if she felt like it!

I got on well with all my patients. It was different being a home help. The job was more caring. I felt concerned for my patients, although the money came in handy.

INA LYNCH

CASTLEMILK CHILDREN'S HOME.

I worked in Castlemilk Children's Home, in the old Castlemilk House, as an all round domestic for four years over twenty years ago. I found it a very good job.

Most of the children came from broken homes and stayed in the Home till they were fostered out or adopted. They attended the local schools and used to get pocket money according to their age : five shillings for teenagers, right down to the babies, who got sixpence. The matron deducted sixpence each week for stamps in the Post Office, so that the children left the home with a bank book.

There was one family of six in the Home who were orphans : the mother had committed suicide and the father was killed in an accident. The youngest, Steven was just a baby and he was there till he was five years old. He was a lovely wee boy, but, unfortunately, he kept running off from school, jumping into railway carriages at Croftfoot and arriving in town and the picture halls! Of course, everybody felt sorry for him and he was sent up north beside his older brother. The staff were all crying when he went away.

I used to take him home with two other wee boys for the weekend. The kids just loved being out of the Home, and it was very hard to take them back again on Monday.

Eventually the Home was pulled down, as Glasgow Corporation couldn't afford the upkeep of it. We used to say, if you needed a plumber, joiner, glazier you could get them anytime in the Home; they were always there doing work.

I hope everything worked out for the best for all the children.

NAN KERR

CHAPTER 8

Church Memories

CASTLEMILK EAST CHURCH

MAMIE MURPHY

I was brought up Baptist, but I went to the Church of Scotland because Jimmy, my husband belonged to that. The Church of Scotland was in Clynder Street just down the street from us. Jimmy was an elder there.

THE BEGINNINGS OF THE CHURCH IN THE WORKMEN'S HUT

When we came up to Castlemilk, there was a workmen's hut on the corner of Machrie Road and Castlemilk Drive, right across from my window. I noticed people going in and out of that hut on Sundays and we found out it was being used for Church of Scotland Services. Because I'm on the west side, I should really have gone to the West Church, but when I came up to Castlemilk, I had the baby and I knew I couldn't go away round there. So my eldest girl used to watch the baby while I went to Church and, when I came back, she went with the other young girl to the Sunday School there. And that's how I became involved with it, sitting in the workmen's hut with all the draughts!

The hut was still used through the week by the workmen who were building the houses round about, but it was cleaned up for the weekends. There was a lovely organ in it that was used on Sundays and just stayed there the rest of the week, none the worse for sharing the space with the workmen.

What we didn't know, when we met on the Sundays, was that we were sharing the hut with more than the workmen. I've heard since, from people whose houses overlooked the hut, that they used to see loads of rats running in and out of it.

Sunday Morning, Machrie Road and Castlemilk Drive with the workmen's hut.

A VISITATION

The first member of the clergy to come to my door was Father Toy, the parish priest, who walked about everywhere and stayed in a five apartment down Castlemilk Drive. He's still spoken of in Castlemilk. He was well-known; he went round chapping every door. The Church of Scotland ministers did the same, but I can't remember who came to mine or whether I just went to church on my own. If you stay away, sometimes you end up not going, so I thought I would start right away, when I came up here. I saw the hut across the road was being used and I knew that was the place to go. That was my first contact with the church.

THE CHURCH FLITS

When I first went across to the hut on a Sunday, it was quite full, but not too full. After a while, there were so many people going that they weren't able to be accommodated inside the hut, so we had to move.

The first place we moved to was Ardencraig Drive, the St Dominics Annexe. It was an ordinary close which was gutted and made into bigger rooms, so it could be used as a school. Arnprior School was created the same way. The Sunday services transferred from the hut to St Dominics at first and then, after a while, to Braeside School.

41

HOUSE CHURCHES

Sunday morning service wasn't all there was in the life of the church at that time. There was another special part of it: house churches. People took turn about to hold the meeting in their house. The minister would come to the house and we had prayer and Bible Study and everybody passed their opinion. Once every two or three months it was in my house. They were very enjoyable.

The only time I really felt embarrassed was once when we had a visit from an American minister, and his talk was all scientific - way above our heads. And we're all sitting and, of course, question time came round. Silence! You could have heard a pin drop. I had a wee budgie that sat at the back and all I heard was :

**"Good old Rangers;
My Daddy's a blue nose".**

I hoped that minister didn't understand. It was a really embarrassing night.

Some nights you had about ten to twelve coming to a meeting like that in a living-room. The children were warned to be quiet and they sat in on the meetings. Not many people had television in those days, so you weren't keeping the children from their TV programmes.

My oldest girl was a great studier and would sit in the room quite a lot of the time studying, and the children could go in beside her. It was mostly people who were in the Church that came to those meetings, although you could invite other people.

The very first Christmas in Castlemilk, in Machrie, the churches organised Christmas parties and there was no distiction made whether people were Catholic or Protestant. People went round and collected money for the parties and they just held them in whatever premises were available.

CHILDREN'S INVOLVEMENT

My children were in everything: the Brownies, Guides; my oldest daughter was a Lifeboy leader and played the piano for the Lifeboys. She played the piano in the church too and was a Sunday School teacher in Braeside School. She was very involved with it. And they all got married in the church.

Castlemilk East,
Temporary church in
workmen's bothy with
organ. 1955

THE NEW CHURCH BUILDING

The Castlemilk East Parish finally built its own church in Barlia Terrace. The foundation was laid in March 1958 and the church was opened in June 1959. The first minister was the Rev. David Reid.

Castlemilk East Church. Laying of the foundation stone.

THE CHURCH OF SCOTLAND'S PLANS

The Church of Scotland looked at all the Glasgow Housing Schemes that were being built at the same time. They had a central organisation called the Church Extension Committee, which operated from Edinburgh but sent its team through. They divided the land up on their own map and decided what would be the shape of the parishes. And the Church Extension Committee appointed ministers and assistants before the houses were even fully built. The congregations were built up by these organisers at the beginning, then, after the church was well established, it applied to became a congregation with 'full status', as they called it. After that, the congregation was able to appoint or 'call' its own ministers. But the first ones were appointed centrally.

Potential population was the criterion used to decide the parishes. Whereas in Drumchapel there are four Church of Scotland parishes and three in Easterhouse, in Castlemilk they decided just to have two, Castlemilk East and Castlemilk West, but that they would put a bigger staff - three - in each church.

The first ministers were both introduced to their parishes on the same day, Mr Reid to the East Parish, Mr McLeod to the West, in an 'induction' service held in the 18th Century Parish Church of Carmunnock.

REV JOHN MILLER

CASTLEMILK WEST PARISH CHURCH

JOHN McKECHNIE

We came to Castlemilk in 1957, when Downcraig Road was just built. We were among the first tenants in Downcraig Road. For about three years, we travelled every Sunday to Calton Church in London Road. Shortly before the birth of our third child we transferred to the local church, Castlemilk West. I had already been an elder in Calton and got transferred to Castlemilk West in May 1960.

Children, Castlemilk West.

THE EARLY DAYS OF CASTLEMILK WEST

The church was built by that time , but, just like Castlemilk East, it started in 1955 in a builder's hut, round about where the bowling green is now in Dougrie Road. As the congregation grew, there wasn't enough room in the hut, so we moved, first to Arnprior School, then to Castleton School in 1956. The foundation stone of the church was laid on 28 September 1957, but the church actually opened and the dedication took place on the 12 December 1959. As far as I know, we had the choice of two sites for the church : where it is now, at the corner of Glenacre Terrace and Carmunnock Road, or on the site where St Margaret Mary's Church was built in the end. The minister thought the site we're on now was better because it was more central.

Castlemilk West Church, laying of the foundation stone, 1957

CHURCH MEMBERSHIP

In the early days, the membership was keen : everybody wanted to join. At one time we had two church services on a Sunday, one at 10.15am and one at 11.30am. But the numbers of the congregation began to dwindle and we only had the one in the morning, though we've always had an evening service. I joined in 1960. By 1961/62, I was an elder and was made Roll Keeper. The roll at that time was thirteen hundred; now it's five hundred and forty. In the late 60's early 70's, a lot of people moved from Castlemilk to the new towns, East Kilbride and Cumbernauld. We lost a lot of our membership through that.

When the church was being built, you were doing something. It was a challenge. Once it was built and established, people didn't lose interest, but there was nothing more to fight for. However, you still had to keep the building; it had to be paid for. You don't get the church for nothing; you have to pay for it over the years. It was about 1970 before the church was actually paid up. It was £1,000 a year for 14 years.

CLUBS AND ASSOCIATIONS:

The Men's Association started in October 1957 and the Women's Guild also started in 57. For the children there were the Girls Brigade (Girls Guildry it was called then), the Boys Brigade and the Lifeboys. The Sunday Schools were held either in Arnprior or Castleton. We used the two schools for a number of years for Sunday School. They would meet in the church for prizegiving or Thanksgiving.

Sunday School in the workmen's hut in Dougrie Road, 1955

GIFTS FOR THE CHURCH

On the 12 December 1959, for the opening, various organisations gifted furniture. The Communion table was gifted by Greenbank Church Women's Guild; the Baptismal font by Stonelaw Church Women's Guild. The Reading Lectern, which is still used, was gifted by Williamwood Church; the Organ presented by the Women's Guild. The Pulpit bible was gifted by the 44A Girls Guildry. At that time, there were so many girls in the Girls Guildry that there was a 44A and a 44B. One met in Castleton School and the other in Arnprior. The Table Lectern was presented by the Bible class; the praise board by the choir; the main entrance door by the Sunday School

The communion table cloth was presented by a Mrs Dool and the pulpit fall by Mrs Steenson, who used to stay in Downcraig Drive. She was a great embroiderer and made it herself. When the Girls Brigade was presented with colours, she embroidered them.

THE WORKING PARTY

We had a great working party. About twenty years ago or so we formed a mens' working party to do all the odd jobs about the church - the plastering and joinery - all the repairs. I remember in the big storm - I think it was 1967 or 68 - we lost half our roof; it was blown off into the grounds. We got the roof repaired and then we decided to paint the church from top to bottom. Everyone helped, from the oldest to the youngest.

ST MARGARET MARY'S CATHOLIC CHURCH

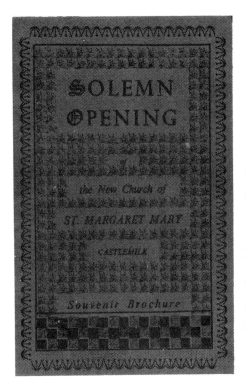

MIMA REID:

Before St Margaret Mary's was established, there was no parish as such in Castlemilk. We had Father Toy, who was responsible for the services for the Catholics in the Castlemilk area. In 1957 the church hadn't been built; the foundation stone hadn't even been laid. They started off with a concert in Cavin Road School and priests that belonged to other parishes as well came to meet the people of Castlemilk.

ST MARGARET MARY'S FIRST PARISH PRIEST

Father Hughes was the first priest in our parish. When he came, they were using a tenement flat in Downcraig Drive - 17 Downcraig Drive - as the church. That's just across the road from where the church is now and Daily Mass was held there. Father Toy and Father O'Flynn held mass there too. Sunday Mass was said in a wooden hut where St Bartholomew's School is now on Cavin Road. But Father Hughes celebrated his first mass in Dougrie Road School, where the Social Work Department is now, in 1957.

THE PARISH GROWS AND THE CHURCH IS BUILT:

The parish was quite small to begin with because the scheme was just being built at the time; the back end of the scheme hadn't been built at all. The building of the church was financed by borrowing from the Diocese - just like going to a Building Society - and, when the church is established the money is paid back over a number of years, possibly twenty years depending on how many parishioners there are, through the collection envelopes and fundraising with Bingo and that sort of thing. That's how the parish got started. They didn't have to wait until they could save the money themselves.

The foundation stone of the church was laid in 1959. But before the church was finished, the hall was able to be used for mass. It's built underneath the church, just like Castlemilk West Church. Some people don't like the hall being underneath because, when there's anything going on in the church itself the sound-proofing isn't all that effective. The idea behind it was to save space.

Church members took no part in the actual building of the church; it was all done by outside contractors. But Father Burke and some of the parishioners did a lot of work on the grounds after the church was built, planted trees and flowers. He was a very hard-working man, still is.

THE SITE OF THE CHURCH:

The church is on an excellent site. We take in up to part of Stravanan so the church is very central. Most people know exactly where St Margaret Mary's is in Castlemilk. It's more or less a landmark, there on the corner of Dougrie Road and Carmunnock Road.

ORGANISATIONS:

The first organisations were the Women's Sacred Heart and the Men's Sacred Heart and they built from there. I don't think there was anything for children at the very beginning. Later on they had a children's club on a Sunday afternoon.

About twenty seven years ago, maybe more, they started up the Ladies Sequence Dancing Club on a Tuesday evening. This is still going strong and some of the original members still go. There's a pensioner's club too, the '66 club', which is open to all denominations, just like the White Heather Club in Castlemilk West Church.

A CALENDAR OF EVENTS IN THE EARLY LIFE
OF ST MARGARET MARY'S

In 1957, Father Hughes celebrated his first mass in Dougrie Road School.

On 15 July, 1957 Daily mass was started in 17 Downcraig Drive.

Father Burke celebrated his first mass on 4 August 1957 in Dougrie Road School.

On Christmas Day 1958 and on New Year's Day, 1959, mass was said in Castleton School.

In 1959, on 5 May, Archbishop Campbell laid the foundation stone of the church.

The first mass to be said in the church hall was on 5 July, 1959. That same evening, the bingo was started.

On the morning of 13 December, 1959, mass was said in the hall. And at noon that day, the church was opened by Archbishop Campbell.

First Communion Day, open-air cermony,
St Margaret Mary's Church

50

LIFE OF THE CHURCH GOES ON;

People worked hard in the early days to build up the church. But there's even more going on nowadays and people do a lot of voluntary work. When the hall was renovated a few years back and the stage taken out, it was parishioners who did all the work. And it was a power of work!

A group of ladies from the church come twice a week on a Friday and a Monday and clean the hall and the church. Mr Tom McAllister and Mr John Bradley, who are both in their eighties, come and dig and look after the church grounds. I think between the two of them they have about 170 years! There's a lot of grounds round the church and it's a power of work, but they still do it.

ST MARTIN'S CHURCH

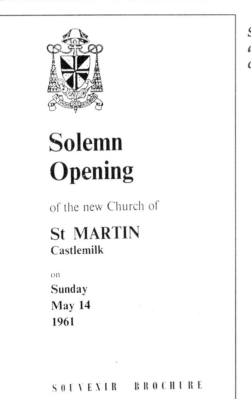

Solemn Opening

of the new Church of

St MARTIN
Castlemilk

on
Sunday
May 14
1961

SOUVENIR BROCHURE

St Martin's Church was built up and opened slightly later than the other three churchs.

51

CHAPTER 9

SHORT BIOGRAPHIES

JOHN JAMIESON

I was born in Sprinburn in 1914. I had two sisters, also born in Sprinburn. We moved to Govanhill in 1925. I started working on the railway in 1930 and worked there for 49 years. I moved to Castlemilk in 1955 because my family needed a bigger house.

MAY MARTIN

I was born in 1926. There was five boys and two girls in my family, all born in Mathieson Street, Oatlands. My first job was as a message girl in A.F. Reids's bakers shop in Mount Florida. I was married in 1950 and moved up to Castlemilk in 1957. I've three of a family.

CECILIA McQUADE

I was born in Camlachie in 1915. I was one of three children. I got married in 1940 and moved to Ardenlee Street and then I moved to Castlemilk in 1956. My first job was working in a shirt factory in 1930. I got six shillings a week.

DUNCAN McCUNN

I was born in Clydebank in 1906. I had two brothers and a sister. I started work on the Glasgow Subway in 1919 - a ticket boy at St George's Cross. I worked on the trams, trolley buses till I retired. I moved to Castlemilk in 1956.

CATHIE COWAN

I was born in March 1916 in Pollokshaws Road. I had three brothers and one sister. My first job was in a baker's shop in Parliamentary Road. I was married in 1947 and lived in London Road. I moved to Castlemilk in 1956.

VICTOR KENNEDY

I was born on 27 April 1913 at Somerville Drive, Mount Florida and later moved to be one of the first tenants in Croftfoot. There were four in our family - one brother and two sisters. I'm an instrument maker to trade, but my first full-time job was conducting buses between Glasgow and the Clyde coast resorts. I've also been a clerk of a municipal golf course, a branch manager with Cochrane's and a travelling salesman. When I married I moved to Govanhill and moved to Castlemilk in July 1977.

JESSIE KENNEDY

I was born in 1914 in Coatbridge. I have two sisters, one born in New Abbey, Dumfries and the other in Coatbridge. My first job was in the dispensary in Rottenrow. I married in 1938. I've lived in Castlemilk since 1977.

MARGARET SLOAN

I was born Margaret McCallum in 1917 in Hutchesontown. I had four sisters and four brothers. I worked in a tailoring factory. I married in 1938 and went to London house searching but came home, got a house on the southside side which was subsequently destroyed by a blast from a land mine in Rutherglen Road. I moved to Castlemilk in 1976.

LILY LOGAN

I was born in 1921 in Kinning Park. I had two sisters. I was a daily maid in a house in Langside Avenue and then I became a waitress. I was married in 1941 and I moved to Castlemilk in 1964.

LIZZIE McSHANE

My mother had a house off Paisley Road, Seaward Street. I had three brothers and three sisters. My first job was in Sloan's Arcade, washing dishes and peeling tatties. My first wage was 7/6d. We worked from eight o'clock in the morning till eleven o'clock at night.

PEGGY MACAULAY

I was born in Oatlands in 1913. I had one brother. My first job was in a licensed grocers in Victoria Road (Lawsons). I got married in 1947 and moved to Castlemilk in 1956 when my son was seven years old.

BESSY LEE

I was born on 4 April 1919 in Germiston. I started work in Collin's Publishers with 9/6d a week in 1933. I got married on 30 December 1939 and had one son. He was fifteen years old when we moved to Castlemilk in May 1956.

JEAN WILLIAMSON

I was born in 1912 in Oatlands. I moved to Castlemilk in 1963. I have two sons both born in Oatlands where I lived when I first got married.

ISA MORGAN

I was born in the Royal Maternity in 23 October 1914. My first job was as a message girl in Curley's Albert Drive. I got 10/- a week. I was married in 1940 and came to Castlemilk in 1957. My daughter was fifteen years old when we came here.

CATHIE SHAW

I was born in Mathieson Street in April 1915. My first job was as a machinist in a shirt factory. I got 6/6d a week. I have one daughter. She was twelve years old when we moved to Castlemilk in 1955.

ISA ROBERTSON

I was born in Cowcaddens in 1923. I had two brothers. My first job was in Treron's, Sauchiehall Street in 1947. I got 8/- a week. I got married in 1942. I have two boys and two girls, all born before we moved to Castlemilk in 1956. The children were fourteen, twelve, ten and two and a half years old.

INA LYNCH

I was born in Pollokshaws on 15 May 1927. I am one of nine children. We moved from Pollokshaws to Carnwadric where we grew up. I started as a machinist in 1951. I got married in 1952. My son was two and a half years old when we moved to Castlemilk in 1958.

ROSE McLEAN

I was born in 1925 in Cowcaddens. I came from seven of a family - three boys, four girls. I left school and worked in 1939 in a clothing manufacturers for 8/- a week. I was married in 1947 and I had six children - three boys, three girls. I came to Castlemilk in 1957 with four children. I had one son and one daughter born in Castlemilk.

MARY DOCHERTY

I was born in Cumberland Street in the south side in April 1922. I was the eldest of eight. My first job was in an olive oil factory. I got 8/- a week in 1931. I got married in 1939. I had three children, I lost my first boy. My other son and daughter were twelve and thirteen years of age when we moved to Castlemilk in 1955 - to the place I'd always wanted to stay, Arnprior.

MAY SHIELDS

I was born in 1919 and stayed with my gran for most of my young life till I married in 1946. My first job was in Twomax, Rutherglen Road. I got 8/- a week in 1933. I came to Castlemilk in 1954 I have two sons.

MARY HENDRY

I was born in 1918, 4 July. I have three of a family, they were all born before I came to Castlemilk in 1956. I have six grand-children and two great-grand children.

AGNES DICKSON

I was born in Sandyfauld Street, Oatlands in 1922. My first job was as a message lassie in Cockburn's the Chemist. I think I got 10/- a week for wages. I moved to Castlemilk in March 1956. My boys were 10 years and 2 years when we came up.

HELEN HENRY

I was born in Dennistoun in 1913. My first job was in a laundry. I moved to Castlemilk in 1956. I had two boys and two girls all born before we came to Castlemilk.

NAN TIERNEY

I was born in Bridgeton in 1927. My first job was in a hosiery factory. I was an 'overlocker'. I moved to Castlemilk in October 1955. I don't have any children.

GEORGE LIND

I was born in Broxburn, West Lothian in March 1909. My first job was as an apprentice dental technician with a starting wage of 2/6d a week. I moved to Castlemilk in 1974 with my son.

JIMMY McCLYMONT

I was born in McAslin Street, Townhead in July 1925. I had a sister and two twin brothers who died. My first job was as a page boy in the George Hotel, Buchanan Street. I got 7/6d a week. I moved to Castlemilk in 1967.

AGNES LEIGHTON

I got married on 27 December 1945 and lived in Oatlands in a single end with outside toilet for twelve years. I moved to Castlemilk in 1958. My daughter was just born. I also had two sons.

SADIE MUIR

I was born in 16 July 1923 in Bridgeton. I first worked in 1937 in a dairy in Duke Street. I got 5/- a week plus meals working from 7.30am -7.30pm Monday - Saturday midday. I moved to Castlemilk in 1964 when my youngest daughter was ten years and the twins (a boy and a girl) were 11 years old.

I.   FOUNDER MEMBERS OF THE HISTORY GROUP
(FORMED SEPTEMBER 1986)

LEFT TO RIGHT : Jessie Kennedy, Duncan McCunn, May
Martin, Vic Kennedy, Cathie Cowan, John Jamieson, Margaret
Sloan.

2.   THE GROUP APRIL 1988

LEFT TO RIGHT : Jean Williamson, Sadie Muir, Bessy Lee,
Agnes Leighton, John Jamieson, May Martin, Agnes Dickson,
Peggy Macaulay, Cathie Shaw, Margaret Cairns.

3.   THE GROUP TODAY - DECEMBER 1989

LEFT TO RIGHT :   May Shields, Nan Tierney, Isa Robertson,
(seated)   Peggy Macaulay, Cathie Shaw, Ina Lynch,
                                 Agnes Dickson, Helen Henry, Jean
                                 Williamson,Isa Morgan.

Guess the Weight
1958